A Far, Far Better Thing To Do

A Lit Lover's Activity Book

by Joelle Herr

Illustrated by Lindsey Spinks

RUNNING PRESS
PHILADELPHIA

For my folks
(my book nerd role models)

Running Press
Hachette Book Group
1290 Avenue of the Americas,
New York, NY 10104
www.runningpress.com
@Running_Press

Printed in the United States of America

First Edition: September 2017

Published by Running Press,
an imprint of Perseus Books, LLC,
a subsidiary of Hachette Book Group, Inc.

The Hachette Speakers Bureau provides a wide range of authors for speaking events. To find out more, go to www.hachettespeakersbureau.com or call (866) 376-6591.

The publisher is not responsible for websites (or their content) that are not owned by the publisher.

Print book cover and interior design by Frances J. Soo Ping Chow.

Library of Congress Control Number: 2017933429

ISBN: 978-0-7624-6253-7

LSC-C

10 9 8 7 6 5 4 3 2 1

INTRODUCTION

If you're reading this, chances are you're a card-carrying (library card, natch), TBR-stacking, unabashed *book nerd*. That you require both hands to count the number of times you've devoured your favorite classic novel. That you own more books than all your other possessions combined. That you have a pet named after a literary character. That you have imagined yourself as mistress of Pemberley. That you know the book Pemberley is from without even having to think about it.

Bibliophile or bookworm, whichever moniker you prefer, if you consider yourself a lit lover, welcome—and get ready to experience and appreciate the classics in a whole new, super-fun, and *interactive* way. On the following pages you'll find a Charles Dickens crossword puzzle, a Flannery O'Connor word search, a *Great Gatsby* connect-the-dots, and a *Moby-Dick* maze, along with drawing, matching, and continue-the-story activities—plus quizzes galore.

So, grab your pens and pencils (regular and colored) and prepare to prove your literary prowess and expand your bookish horizons.

In the Beginning

YOU MAY CALL YOURSELF A LIT LOVER,
BUT HOW WELL DO YOU KNOW THE
OPENING LINES OF SOME OF LITERATURE'S
MOST ICONIC WORKS?

Test your knowledge with this matching game.

· · ·

_____ **1.** *Heart of Darkness* by Joseph Conrad

_____ **2.** *This Side of Paradise* by F. Scott Fitzgerald

_____ **3.** *Jane Eyre* by Charlotte Brontë

_____ **4.** *The Portrait of a Lady* by Henry James

_____ **5.** *The Scarlet Letter* by Nathaniel Hawthorne

_____ **6.** *David Copperfield* by Charles Dickens

_____ **7.** *Little Women* by Louisa May Alcott

_____ **8.** *Moby-Dick* by Herman Melville

A. "Call me Ishmael."

B. "Whether I shall turn out to be the hero of my life, or whether that station will be held by anybody else, these pages must show."

C. "*The Nellie*, a cruising yawl, swung to her anchor without a flutter of the sails, and was at rest."

D. "'Christmas won't be Christmas without any presents,' grumbled Jo, lying on the rug."

E. "Amory Blaine inherited from his mother every trait, except the stray inexpressible few, that made him worthwhile."

F. "Under certain circumstances, there are few hours in life more agreeable than the hour dedicated to the ceremony known as afternoon tea."

G. "There was no possibility of taking a walk that day."

H. "A throng of bearded men, in sad-colored garments and grey steeple-crowned hats, intermixed with women, some wearing hoods, and others bareheaded, was assembled in front of a wooden edifice, the door of which was heavily timbered with oak, and studded with iron spikes."

ANSWERS ON PAGE 94.

There She Blows!

Help Ahab and his *Pequod* crew navigate the cold,
relentless seas to track down Moby-Dick.

Or, start from the bottom right to help Moby-Dick catch up with the Pequod and mess with the unhinged captain whose leg he once snacked upon.

SOLUTION ON PAGE 103.

Vile Villains

CHEATERS, MURDERERS, SCOUNDRELS,
KIDNAPPERS, AND ALL-AROUND BAD GUYS.

Match these unforgettable characters with
their skin-crawling, nightmare-inducing descriptions.

———◆———

_____ **1.** The Martians from *The War of the Worlds* by H. G. Wells

_____ **2.** Captain Hook from *Peter and Wendy* by J. M. Barrie

_____ **3.** Mr. Hyde from *The Strange Case of Dr. Jekyll
and Mr. Hyde* by Robert Louis Stevenson

_____ **4.** Bill Sikes from *Oliver Twist* by Charles Dickens

_____ **5.** Mr. Wickham from *Pride and Prejudice* by Jane Austen

_____ **6.** Count Dracula from *Dracula* by Bram Stoker

A. "His appearance was greatly in his favor; he had all the best part of beauty, a fine countenance, a good figure, and very pleasing address. The introduction was followed up on his side by a happy readiness of conversation—a readiness at the same time perfectly correct and unassuming."

B. "He gave an impression of deformity without any nameable malformation, he had a displeasing smile, he had borne himself to the lawyer with a sort of murderous mixture of timidity and boldness, and he spoke with a husky, whispering and somewhat broken voice."

C. "There was a mouth under the eyes, the lipless brim of which quivered and panted, and dropped saliva. The whole creature heaved and pulsated convulsively."

D. "He had a brown hat on his head, and a dirty belcher handkerchief round his neck: with the long frayed ends of which he smeared the beer from his face as he spoke. He disclosed, when he had done so, a broad heavy countenance with a beard of three days' growth, and two scowling eyes; one of which displayed various parti-colored symptoms of having been recently damaged by a blow."

E. "In person he was cadaverous and blackavized, and his hair was dressed in long curls, which at a little distance looked like black candles, and gave a singularly threatening expression to his handsome countenance. His eyes were of the blue of the forget-me-not, and of a profound melancholy."

F. "His eyebrows were very massive, almost meeting over the nose, and with bushy hair that seemed to curl in its own profusion. The mouth, so far as I could see it under the heavy moustache, was fixed and rather cruel-looking, with peculiarly sharp white teeth; these protruded over the lips, whose remarkable ruddiness showed astonishing vitality in a man of his years."

ANSWERS ON PAGE 94.

Hemingway Hunt

HEMINGWAY WAS INFAMOUSLY ECONOMICAL
WITH WORDS, BUT THOSE HE USED
REALLY PACKED A PUNCH.

See if you can track down the words below that are
associated with Papa and his works.

```
K O Q W G W T A P S X P A K W
V W R B S S L A A W Z Y I O D
X F U L E E P W R A H L M X S
I M J W L A N E I K I E N H L
F P Y W P W Q R S M N L N Q H
S E Z Y E L H S A T T E R B T
K O B V M Q U N U B Z L T Y H
U Y G O A N J X H V E J V A G
N S P L X A I N M F U K P K I
I G G H R I N A Q P B D A A F
X Z R O G F N H P M Y R A J L
C A T S H O W G S S J A V N L
M A R L I N O H C A M E C G U
F J N G N X A R W H S B R T B
Z I S V S K S A Z Y N M D R H
```

marlin	Kilimanjaro	women	cats
bullfight	Jake Barnes	boxing	beard
Paris	Brett Ashley	macho	
Papa	Key West	Spain	

SOLUTION ON PAGE 109.

Spinster: Yea or Nay?

SOME OF LITERATURE'S MOST ACCOMPLISHED AND ADMIRED
WOMEN NEVER MARRIED, CHOOSING NOT TO BE DISTRACTED BY
WHAT ONE SUCH CONVENTION-SHUNNER* REFERRED
TO AS "CONJUGAL AND MATERNAL AFFECTIONS."

Test your knowledge of literary spinsters
(aka way-ahead-of-their-time, badass authoresses) below.

AUTHORESSES	MARRIED	SPINSTER
1. Flannery O'Connor		
2. Emily Dickinson		
3. Virginia Woolf		
4. Jane Austen		
5. Charlotte Brontë		
6. George Eliot		
7. Edith Wharton		
8. Harper Lee		
9. Shirley Jackson		
10. Eudora Welty		
11. Louisa May Alcott		
12. Daphne du Maurier		

ANSWERS ON PAGE 94.

*Do you know which one? She's identified in the answers. Give yourself an extra point—or at least a pat
on the back—if you get it right.

Swept Off Her Feet

*She had raised herself from the ground, but her foot
had been twisted in her fall, and she was scarcely able to stand.
The gentleman offered his services; and perceiving
that her modesty declined what her situation rendered
necessary, took her up in his arms without farther delay,
and carried her down the hill.*

Grab your colored pencils and add some color to this pivotal,
oh-so-romantic scene from Jane Austen's *Sense and Sensibility*.

Marry, Kill, Do

LITERATURE IS FULL OF MEMORABLE CHARACTERS WHO'VE MADE READERS SWOON, WEEP, FUME—AND EVERYTHING IN BETWEEN—FOR AGES.

Decide which of these fictional dudes you'd like to marry, which you'd like to kill, and which you'd like to do.

CHARACTERS	M	K	D
MISTERS			
Mr. Rochester from *Jane Eyre*			
Mr. Darcy from *Pride and Prejudice*			
Mr. Bingley from *Pride and Prejudice*			
BROODERS			
Jake Barnes from *The Sun Also Rises*			
Heathcliff from *Wuthering Heights*			
Maxim de Winter from *Rebecca*			
DO-GOODERS			
Atticus Finch from *To Kill a Mockingbird*			
Edward Ferrars from *Sense and Sensibility*			
Gilbert Blythe from *Anne of Green Gables*			
ADVENTURERS			
Edmond Dantès from *The Count of Monte Cristo*			
Aragorn from *The Lord of the Rings* series			
Ishmael from *Moby-Dick*			
CADS			
Alec d'Urberville from *Tess of the d'Urbervilles*			
Tom Buchanan from *The Great Gatsby*			
George Wickham from *Pride and Prejudice*			

Picture It

"Miss Brooke had that kind of beauty
which seems to be thrown into relief by poor dress."

THIS EVOCATIVE FIRST LINE FROM GEORGE ELIOT'S *MIDDLEMARCH*
INTRODUCES DOROTHEA BROOKE IN ALL HER 1830s BEAUTY.

Time for you to tap into your inner fashion designer and
draw Dorothea's "poor dress."

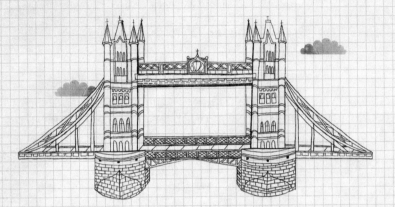

A Dickensian World

CHARLES DICKENS'S TWENTY-TWO NOVELS FEATURE
A CAST OF NEARLY ONE THOUSAND NAMED CHARACTERS—
INCLUDING PIP, EBENEZER SCROOGE, AND THE ARTFUL DODGER.

Test your Dickens IQ by completing this crossword filled with
clues relating to Boz and his works.

ACROSS

4. This queen ruled during Dickens's life
6. Oliver Twist villain
9. Tiny _____
10. *Great Expectations* vindictive spinster
12. Oliver dares to ask for some more of this
13. *David Copperfield* schemer
14. Pip's first name
15. "It was the best of _____, it was the worst of _____."

DOWN

1. *Our Mutual* _____
2. "It is a far, far better thing that I _____"
3. *The* _____ *Papers*
5. *A Tale of Two Cities* setting
7. Scrooge's deceased partner
8. Nell Trent's grandfather is addicted to this
11. *The Old Curiosity* _____
14. Place of Amy "Little" Dorrit's birth

SOLUTION ON PAGE 98.

Write On!

"Tom!"

Continue the story from this attention-grabbing opening line
from Mark Twain's *The Adventures of Tom Sawyer*. Who's Tom? Who's
yelling his name, and why? Where and when is this going on?

If you run out of room, get thee to a computer or notebook and keep going.

Who Played Whom?

ALCOHOLISM, SUICIDE, INFIDELITY, PRISON. WE'RE TALKING THE
REAL LIVES OF WRITERS, NOT PLOT POINTS FROM THEIR NOVELS.

Match the infamous scribes below with the actors
who played them in silver-screen biopics.

• • •

_____ 1. John Keats and Herman Melville

_____ 2. Sylvia Plath

_____ 3. T. S. Eliot

_____ 4. David Foster Wallace

_____ 5. Dorothy Parker

_____ 6. Jane Austen

_____ 7. C. S. Lewis

_____ 8. William Shakespeare

_____ 9. Oscar Wilde

_____ 10. Virginia Woolf and Martha Gellhorn

_____ 11. J. M. Barrie

_____ 12. Truman Capote

_____ 13. Beatrix Potter

_____ 14. Allen Ginsberg and Hart Crane

A. James Franco

B. Gwyneth Paltrow

C. Jennifer Jason Leigh

D. Ben Whishaw

E. Willem Dafoe

F. Johnny Depp

G. Anne Hathaway

H. Renée Zellweger

I. Stephen Fry

J. Philip Seymour Hoffman

K. Nicole Kidman

L. Anthony Hopkins

M. Jason Segel

N. Joseph Fiennes

ANSWERS ON PAGE 94.

Standin' on the Dock
of the Bay

Connect the dots to reveal a memorable scene of obsession and longing
from F. Scott Fitzgerald's *The Great Gatsby*.

SOLUTION ON PAGE TK.

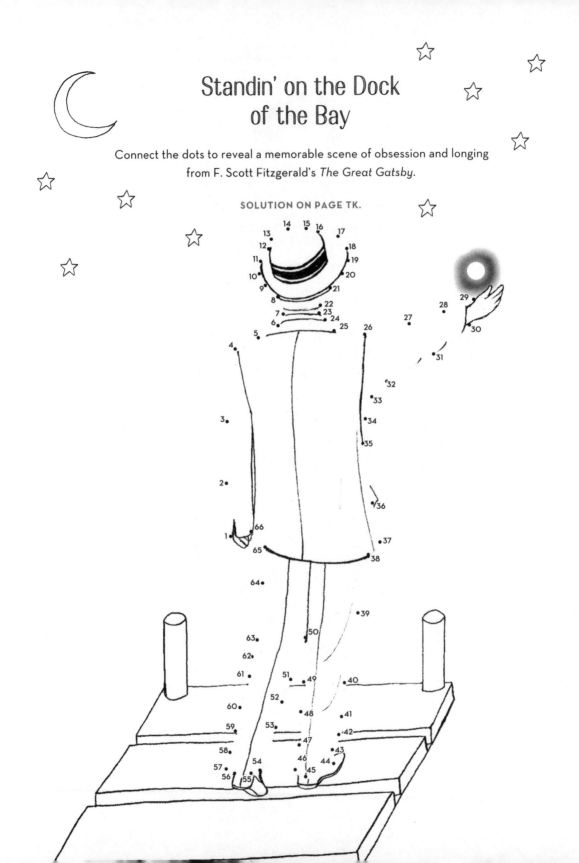

Title Trivia

THE TITLES OF THE CLASSICS ARE SO INGRAINED THAT IT'S
HARD TO IMAGINE THAT SOME WERE LAST-MINUTE CHANGES
BEFORE PUBLICATION—SOME EVEN OCCURRING *AFTER*
THE INITIAL PRINTING.

Match the working title to the iconic work
it would ultimately become.

———◆———

_____ **1.** Too Late, Beloved!

_____ **2.** Fiesta

_____ **3.** The High-Bouncing Lover

_____ **4.** Strangers from Within

_____ **5.** The Kingdom by the Sea

_____ **6.** Something That Happened

_____ **7.** The Year of the Rose

_____ **8.** First Impressions

_____ **9.** They Don't Build Statues
to Businessmen

_____ **10.** Before This Anger

A. *Roots* by Alex Haley

B. *Pride and Prejudice* by Jane Austen

C. *Tess of the d'Urbervilles*
by Thomas Hardy

D. *Lord of the Flies* by William Golding

E. *Valley of the Dolls*
by Jacqueline Susann

F. *The House of Mirth* by Edith Wharton

G. *Lolita* by Vladimir Nabokov

H. *The Sun Also Rises*
by Ernest Hemingway

I. *Of Mice and Men* by John Steinbeck

J. *The Great Gatsby*
by F. Scott Fitzgerald

ANSWERS ON PAGE 94.

Bloomsday Meandering

It's the morning of June 16, 1904. Accompany Leopold Bloom—from James Joyce's *Ulysses*—on his day around Dublin, starting and ending at his home at 7 Eccles Street.

SOLUTION ON PAGE 103.

Love Match

SURE, DARCY MAKES YOU SWOON. JOIN THE CLUB. (SERIOUSLY,
THERE *ARE* ACTUAL MR. DARCY FAN CLUBS OUT THERE.)
BUT HOW PROFICIENT ARE YOU AT IDENTIFYING
LITERARY LOVE DECLARATIONS?

Match each dashing hero with his heartfelt profession.

• • •

_____ 1. "In vain have I struggled. It will not do. My feelings will not be repressed. You must allow me to tell you how ardently I admire and love you."

_____ 2. "I want you to have your own thoughts and ideas and feelings, even when I hold you in my arms."

_____ 3. "I do love nothing in the world so well as you—is not that strange?"

_____ 4. "You pierce my soul. I am half agony, half hope. Tell me not that I am too late, that such precious feelings are gone for ever. I offer myself to you again with a heart even more your own than when you almost broke it, eight years and a half ago."

_____ 5. "You—you strange, you almost unearthly thing!—I love as my own flesh. You—poor and obscure, and small and plain as you are—I entreat to accept me as a husband."

_____ 6. "You should be kissed and often, and by someone who knows how."

A. George Emerson to Lucy Honeychurch in *A Room with a View*

B. Mr. Darcy to Elizabeth Bennet in *Pride and Prejudice*

C. Rhett Butler to Scarlet O'Hara in *Gone with the Wind*

D. Captain Wentworth to Anne Elliot in *Persuasion*

E. Mr. Rochester to Jane Eyre in *Jane Eyre*

F. Benedick to Beatrice in *Much Ado about Nothing*

ANSWERS ON PAGE 94.

A Good Word Is Hard to Find

THE REVELATORY AND INSIGHTFUL WORKS
OF SELF-DESCRIBED "HERMIT NOVELIST"
FLANNERY O'CONNOR ARE SINGULAR IN THEIR TONE,
THEMES, AND KEEN WIT.

Locate these words associated with her life
and writings in the grid below.

```
C V R Q Q T D S I L Z P R T E
X A R N W S N O M O N Z N N G
Z G Q D T O S V O E W D G E R
C A T H O L I C H L C A L L E
N O I T A L E V E R B P A O V
P S R N B S Y F D N E E S I N
E A O O A C H U S A G Q S V O
C V R S I M M S C A M I E I C
X H V H O Y D O X I E L S S W
F Y T T D U C O Y A D D O B L
W O O R P K T I O R H A W H N
G N A C M P Z H P G T T Y V U
R Y J A I G R O E G L D I O J
Q F T R H T F A F R S M F M C
B A R W S L C Y X G N N K O I
```

glasses

Wise Blood

peacock

Georgia

converge

good man

violent

gothic

revelation

Iowa

cartoons

Catholic

Yaddo

Southern

SOLUTION ON PAGE 109.

Odd Jobs

EVEN WRITERS GOTTA PAY THE BILLS.

Match these authors with the day jobs they held to make ends meet
before hitting the big time—some even after!

* * *

_____ **1.** Kurt Vonnegut

_____ **2.** Wallace Stevens

_____ **3.** Herman Melville

_____ **4.** J. D. Salinger

_____ **5.** Jaqueline Susann

_____ **6.** William Carlos Williams

_____ **7.** Toni Morrison

_____ **8.** Harper Lee

_____ **9.** John Steinbeck

A. teacher and editor

B. insurance executive

C. cruise activities director

D. actor

E. customs inspector

F. car dealer

G. airline ticket agent

H. tour guide

I. doctor

ANSWERS ON PAGE 94.

A Young Man of Extraordinary Personal Beauty

The studio was filled with the rich odor of roses, and when the light summer wind stirred amidst the trees of the garden, there came through the open door the heavy scent of the lilac, or the more delicate perfume of the pink-flowering thorn.

From the corner of the divan of Persian saddle-bags on which he was lying, smoking, as was his custom, innumerable cigarettes, Lord Henry Wotton could just catch the gleam of the honey-sweet and honey-colored blossoms of a laburnum, whose tremulous branches seemed hardly able to bear the burden of a beauty so flamelike as theirs. . . .

In the center of the room, clamped to an upright easel, stood the full-length portrait of a young man of extraordinary personal beauty, and in front of it, some little distance away, was sitting the artist himself, Basil Hallward, whose sudden disappearance some years ago caused, at the time, such public excitement and gave rise to so many strange conjectures.

• • •

Add some color to the lush, Victorian-era parlor described in the opening of Oscar Wilde's *The Picture of Dorian Gray*.

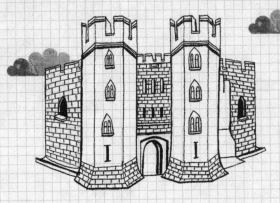

Much Ado about Shakespeare

SHAKESPEARE PENNED A WHOPPING THIRTY-EIGHT PLAYS,
154 SONNETS, AND A COUPLE OF EPIC NARRATIVE POEMS IN
HIS RELATIVELY SHORT LIFETIME OF FIFTY-TWO YEARS.

Test your Shakespeare IQ by completing this crossword filled
with clues and answers relating to the Bard and his works.

ACROSS

3. Hamlet's mom

5. Othello villain

6. *The Tempest* setting

8. Hot-tempered son of the Earl of Northumberland

10. This portly sidekick appears in three of Shakespeare's plays

13. "Double, double toil and _____"

14. Romeo and Juliet city

DOWN

1. "My kingdom for a _____"

2. Julius Caesar traitor

3. Regan and _____

4. "Now is the winter of our _____."

7. "Shall I _____ thee to a summer's day?"

9. "All that _____ is not gold."

11. *Midsummer*'s "shrewd and knavish sprite"

12. The _____ Theatre

15. Cleopatra's cause of death

SOLUTION ON PAGE 99.

Parting Is
Such Sweet Sorrow

SOME CHARACTERS EXIT THE PAGE WITH
AN EXCLAMATION, OTHERS WITH A WHISPER.

Test your knowledge of notable departures by matching
these final words to their speakers.

• • •

_____ 1. "The rest is silence."

_____ 2. "Madman! Madman! I tell you that she now stands without
the door."

_____ 3. "Lord, forgive me everything."

_____ 4. "Demand me nothing: what you know, you know. From this
time forth I never will speak word."

_____ 5. "I am ready."

_____ 6. "It isn't fair, it isn't right."

_____ 7. "It is a far, far better thing that I do, than I have ever done;
it is a far, far better rest that I go to than I have ever known."

_____ 8. "Well, good-by."

_____ 9. "The horror! The horror!"

_____ 10. "Thus, I give up the spear!"

A. Tess Durbeyfield from *Tess of the d'Urbervilles* by Thomas Hardy

B. Captain Kurtz from *Heart of Darkness* by Joseph Conrad

C. Roderick Usher from *The Fall of the House of Usher* by Edgar Allan Poe

D. Captain Ahab from *Moby-Dick* by Herman Melville

E. Sydney Carton from *A Tale of Two Cities* by Charles Dickens

F. Othello from *Othello* by William Shakespeare

G. Jay Gatsby from *The Great Gatsby* by F. Scott Fitzgerald

H. Hamlet from *Hamlet* by William Shakespeare

I. Tessie Hutchinson from "The Lottery" by Shirley Jackson

J. Anna Karenina from *Anna Karenina* by Leo Tolstoy

ANSWERS ON PAGE 94.

Legendary Lit Disses

LITERARY GENIUS IS OFTEN ACCOMPANIED BY
SIGNIFICANT EGO, WHICH HAS LED TO SOME MONUMENTAL
RIVALRIES, WRITER-TO-WRITER PUTDOWNS,
AND EVEN OCCASIONAL FISTICUFFS.

Test your knowledge of lit-based spats, disses, and
the like with this multiple-choice quiz.

---

1. William Faulkner griped about this contemporary: "He has never been known to use a word that might send a reader to the dictionary."

    A. Ernest Hemingway

    B. James Joyce

    C. F. Scott Fitzgerald

    D. John Dos Passos

2. Ouch! Truman Capote said of this writer's work, "That's not writing. That's typing."

    A. J. D. Salinger

    B. Gertrude Stein

    C. Jack Kerouac

    D. Philip Roth

3. D. H. Lawrence described this writer's work as, "Nothing but old fags [cigarettes] and cabbage stumps of quotations from the Bible and the rest stewed in the juice of deliberate, journalistic dirty-mindedness."

    A. John Updike

    B. Vladimir Nabokov

    C. Flannery O'Connor

    D. James Joyce

4. Dylan Thomas called this poet, "the great Frost of literature, the verbose, the humorless, the platitudinary reporter of Nature in her dullest moods."

    A. Percy Shelley

    B. John Milton

    C. William Wordsworth

    D. Walt Whitman

5. Mary McCarthy said of this writer, "Every word she writes is a lie, including 'and' and 'the.'" A lawsuit for libel followed.

    A. Dorothy Parker

    B. Lillian Hellman

    C. Ayn Rand

    D. Shirley Jackson

ANSWERS ON PAGE 94.

Every Artistic Sin

I never saw a worse paper in my life.

One of those sprawling flamboyant patterns committing every artistic sin.

It is dull enough to confuse the eye in following, pronounced enough to constantly irritate and provoke study, and when you follow the lame uncertain curves for a little distance they suddenly commit suicide—plunge off at outrageous angles, destroy themselves in unheard of contradictions.

• • •

Channel your inner artist and draw the "sprawling flamboyant" wallcovering design described in Charlotte Perkins Gilman's "The Yellow Wallpaper." Color it, too, if you dare. Just don't stare at it too long, or madness might ensue!

Shakespeare, Dickens, or Joyce?

SHAKESPEARE, DICKENS, AND JOYCE WERE CLEAR LOVERS
OF THE FLUIDITY OF LANGUAGE, COINING MANY
A WORD IN THEIR WORKS.

Test your etymological know-how by identifying whether the following
originated* with the Bard, Boz, or the modernist maestro.

• • •

1. boredom _____

2. zany _____

3. magnetic slumber _____

4. rant _____

5. whenceness _____

6. doormat _____

7. quark _____

8. bedazzled _____

9. butterfingers _____

10. dreck _____

ANSWERS ON PAGE 94.

*Definitive word origins are tricky to track down. The ones in this activity are conventionally agreed
upon, though there are dissenters.

Write On!

"Alice was beginning to get very tired of sitting by her sister on the bank, and of having nothing to do."

Continue your own version of the story after this opening line from Lewis Carroll's *Alice's Adventures in Wonderland*. Who is Alice? Why is she sitting on the bank, and what is it that she wishes she were doing?

If you run out of room, get thee to a computer or notebook and keep going.

Into the Woods

Connect the dots to reveal where Henry David Thoreau moved
in the summer of 1845, wishing "to live deliberately, to front only the essential
facts of life, and see if I could not learn what it had to teach, and not,
when I came to die, discover that I had not lived."

SOLUTION ON PAGE 96.

Let's Get Visual

Can you decipher the titles of eight classics
from these series of emojis?

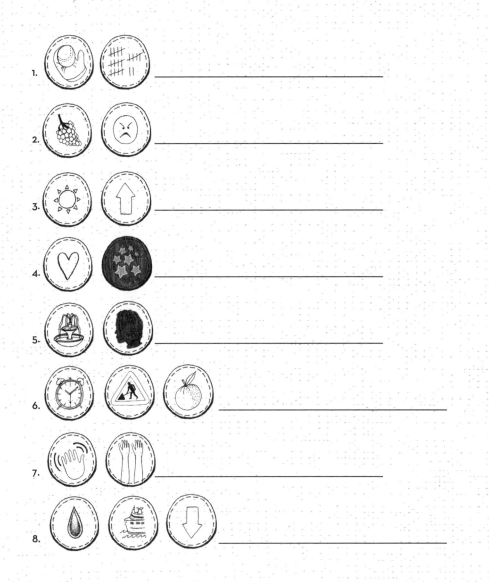

1. _____

2. _____

3. _____

4. _____

5. _____

6. _____

7. _____

8. _____

ANSWERS ON PAGE 95.

Literary Lotharios

WHO DOESN'T LOVE A BAD BOY—ESPECIALLY
ONE WIELDING A WICKED WAY WITH WORDS?

Match the notorious heartbreakers below with their off-the-page exploits.

_____ 1. Ernest Hemingway   _____ 4. Charles Dickens

_____ 2. Norman Mailer   _____ 5. Henry Miller

_____ 3. Lord Byron   _____ 6. Giacomo Girolamo Casanova

A. This irresistible Romantic was stunningly gorgeous and described by one lover as "mad, bad, and dangerous to know."

B. This tough-but-diminutive guy boasted two Pulitzers and six wives.

C. This mega-successful writer was a fortysomething married father of nine when he embarked on a secret relationship with a teen actress. The affair would last until his death, thirteen years later.

D. Though this ladies' man was well known for his machismo, his love letters to his four (different) wives were surprisingly tender.

E. He detailed amorous encounters with more than 120 women in his memoirs—the original manuscript of which sold for $9.6 million at auction in 2010.

F. This racy wordsmith married five times, each wife younger than the previous one. His last wife, whom he divorced the year before his death, was nearly fifty years his junior.

ANSWERS ON PAGE 95.

On the Road

Join Sal and Dean for their journey from New York to San Francisco, making some stops along the way. Just be sure to avoid Squaresville!

SOLUTION ON PAGE 104.

Marry, Kill, Do

THE BARD'S PLAYS FEATURE MORE THAN ONE THOUSAND
CHARACTERS, RANGING FROM MURDEROUS ROYALS TO
FEISTY SPRITES TO LOVESICK TEENS.

Decide which of these Shakespearean leading men you'd like to marry,
which you'd like to kill, and which you'd like to do.

CHARACTERS	M	K	D
VILLAINS			
Iago from *Othello*			
Shylock from *The Merchant of Venice*			
Claudius from *Hamlet*			
GOOFS			
Falstaff from *Henry IV, Part 1* and *Part 2*, and *The Merry Wives of Windsor*			
Bottom from *A Midsummer Night's Dream*			
Puck from *A Midsummer Night's Dream*			
BROODERS			
Hamlet from *Hamlet*			
Othello from *Othello*			
Macbeth from *Macbeth*			
ROYALTY			
King Lear from *King Lear*			
Henry VIII from *Henry VIII*			
Richard III from *Richard III*			
ROMANTICS			
Antony from *Antony and Cleopatra*			
Romeo from *Romeo and Juliet*			
Benedick from *Much Ado about Nothing*			

Renaissance Fare

DURING THE 1920s AND '30s, HARLEM WAS A CULTURAL MECCA
FOR WRITERS, ARTISTS, AND MUSICIANS WHO GAVE
NEW VOICE TO THE BLACK EXPERIENCE.

In this word search, seek out the following people, places,
and things associated with the Harlem Renaissance.

```
N  R  C  X  P  R  F  H  Z  S  V  M  V  T  A
C  O  W  U  E  K  U  Y  L  I  Y  P  L  R  Z
F  K  I  M  L  G  G  M  N  S  H  R  Q  I  F
L  G  O  T  H  T  O  Z  A  I  U  I  L  F  Q
M  O  W  E  A  K  U  E  K  R  R  D  N  Y  O
T  O  S  J  X  R  K  R  X  C  S  E  M  I  Z
B  Y  T  W  I  A  G  C  E  E  T  C  F  J  F
J  Y  Z  D  E  T  W  I  S  H  O  V  D  U  I
K  P  R  P  U  D  Q  B  M  T  N  J  I  X  N
M  B  S  T  S  B  G  F  B  T  D  D  R  U  E
G  A  R  V  E  Y  O  Q  I  P  A  Z  P  G  L
R  F  Z  F  O  P  I  Z  G  I  E  U  A  L
K  C  O  L  X  J  P  J  S  S  C  E  R  T  U
I  D  E  N  T  I  T  Y  H  A  A  T  V  G  C
H  A  M  E  L  R  A  H  K  Y  R  Q  Z  J  S
```

culture	poetry	speakeasy	Great Migration
Hurston	Cullen	identity	Du Bois
Hughes	Toomer	Garvey	
Harlem	The Crisis	pride	

SOLUTION ON PAGE 110.

Hit or Flop?

**MANY NOW-ICONIC CLASSICS WERE
COMMERCIAL AND CRITICAL FLOPS WHEN
THEY WERE FIRST PUBLISHED.**

Prove your prowess as a true lit aficionado by identifying
whether these tomes were initial hits or flops.

TITLE	HIT	FLOP
1. *Moby-Dick* by Herman Melville		
2. *The Wonderful Wizard of Oz* by L. Frank Baum		
3. *The Great Gatsby* by F. Scott Fitzgerald		
4. *Walden* by Henry David Thoreau		
5. *Gone with the Wind* by Margaret Mitchell		
6. *Uncle Tom's Cabin* by Harriet Beecher Stowe		
7. *Wuthering Heights* by Emily Brontë		
8. *Little Women* by Louisa May Alcott		
9. *Lord of the Flies* by William Golding		
10. *Native Son* by Richard Wright		

ANSWERS ON PAGE 95.

Write On!

I confess that when first I made acquaintance with Charles Strickland I never for a moment discerned that there was in him anything out of the ordinary.

Continue the story after this opening line from W. Somerset Maugham's *The Moon and Sixpence.* You could delve into where and under what circumstances the narrator met Charles, or you could dive right into how and when the narrator learned that initial impressions often turn out to be wrong.

If you run out of room, get thee to a computer or notebook and keep going.

Northanger Savvy

CALL YOURSELF A TRUE JANEITE?

Put your Austen IQ to the test with this crossword filled
with tidbits from her life and works.

ACROSS

2. The play within *Mansfield Park*:
Lovers' ____

4. *Pride and Prejudice* scoundrel

8. "To be fond of ____ was a certain
step towards falling in love."

10. *Sense and Sensibility* scoundrel

11. Darcy's BFF

15. Elinor and ____

DOWN

1. Catherine Morland's guilty
pleasure: ____ novels

3. Darcy's estate

5. Frederick Wentworth's
profession

6. Emma Woodhouse's hobby

7. "A large ____ is the best recipe
for happiness I ever heard of."

9. "You pierce my soul. I am half
agony, half ____"

11. *Persuasion* and *Northanger
Abbey* setting

12. Site of Louisa Musgrove's fall

13. The studious Bennet sister

14. "A single man in possession
of a good fortune must be in
want of a ____"

SOLUTION ON PAGE 100.

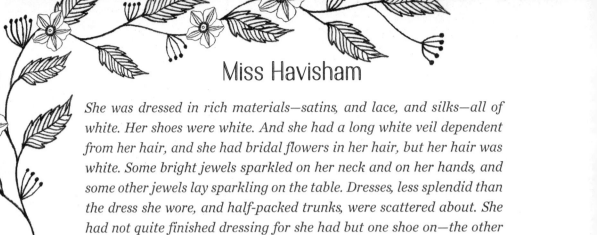

Miss Havisham

She was dressed in rich materials—satins, and lace, and silks—all of white. Her shoes were white. And she had a long white veil dependent from her hair, and she had bridal flowers in her hair, but her hair was white. Some bright jewels sparkled on her neck and on her hands, and some other jewels lay sparkling on the table. Dresses, less splendid than the dress she wore, and half-packed trunks, were scattered about. She had not quite finished dressing for she had but one shoe on—the other was on the table near her hand—her veil was but half arranged, her watch and chain were not put on, and some lace for her bosom lay with those trinkets, and with her handkerchief, and gloves, and some flowers, and a prayer-book, all confusedly heaped about the looking-glass.

• • •

Grab your colored pencils and add some color to this description of literature's most infamous (and unhinged) spinster, Miss Havisham from Charles Dickens's *Great Expectations*.

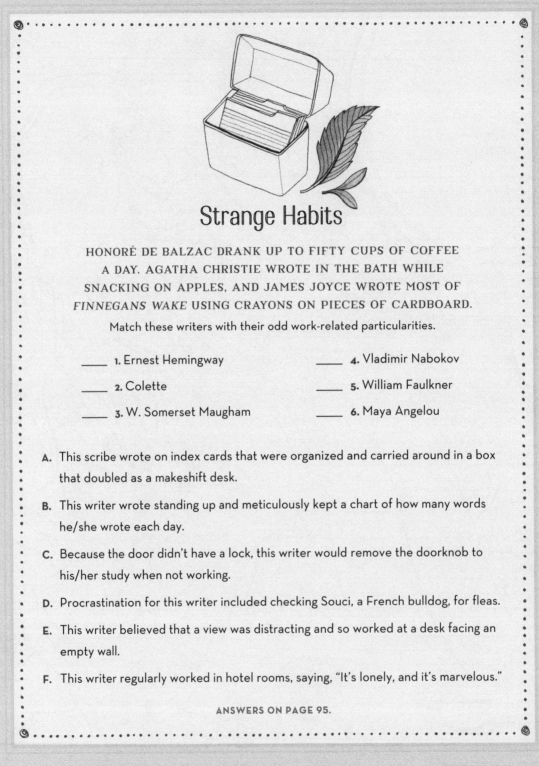

Strange Habits

HONORÉ DE BALZAC DRANK UP TO FIFTY CUPS OF COFFEE
A DAY. AGATHA CHRISTIE WROTE IN THE BATH WHILE
SNACKING ON APPLES, AND JAMES JOYCE WROTE MOST OF
FINNEGANS WAKE USING CRAYONS ON PIECES OF CARDBOARD.

Match these writers with their odd work-related particularities.

_____ 1. Ernest Hemingway

_____ 2. Colette

_____ 3. W. Somerset Maugham

_____ 4. Vladimir Nabokov

_____ 5. William Faulkner

_____ 6. Maya Angelou

A. This scribe wrote on index cards that were organized and carried around in a box that doubled as a makeshift desk.

B. This writer wrote standing up and meticulously kept a chart of how many words he/she wrote each day.

C. Because the door didn't have a lock, this writer would remove the doorknob to his/her study when not working.

D. Procrastination for this writer included checking Souci, a French bulldog, for fleas.

E. This writer believed that a view was distracting and so worked at a desk facing an empty wall.

F. This writer regularly worked in hotel rooms, saying, "It's lonely, and it's marvelous."

ANSWERS ON PAGE 95.

War and (No) Peace

FEW TOPICS ARE MORE FERTILE FOR A WRITER THAN WARTIME,
SO IT'S NO WONDER THAT MANY CLASSICS ARE SET DURING
TUMULTUOUS TIMES OF CONFLICT.

Match each of these books with the war against
which its narrative unfolds.

War and Peace by Leo Tolstoy	French and Indian War (1754–63)
A Tale of Two Cities by Charles Dickens	French Revolution (1789–99)
All Quiet on the Western Front by Erich Maria Remarque	Napoleonic Wars (1803–15)
Catch-22 by Joseph Heller	American Civil War (1861–65)
The Last of the Mohicans by James Fenimore Cooper	World War I (1914–18)
Gone with the Wind by Margaret Mitchell	Spanish Civil War (1936–39)
For Whom the Bell Tolls by Ernest Hemingway	World War II (1939–45)

SOLUTION ON PAGE 106.

Mars Attacks

A big, grayish rounded bulk, the size, perhaps, of a bear, was rising slowly and painfully out of the cylinder. . . . Two large dark-colored eyes were regarding me steadfastly. The mass that framed them, the head of the thing, was rounded, and had, one might say, a face. There was a mouth under the eyes, the lipless brim of which quivered and panted, and dropped saliva. . . . A lank, tentacular appendage gripped the edge of the cylinder, another swayed in the air.

Steady your hand—surely shaking from H. G. Wells's horrifying description from *The War of the Worlds*—and draw the grotesque Martian emerging from its ship.

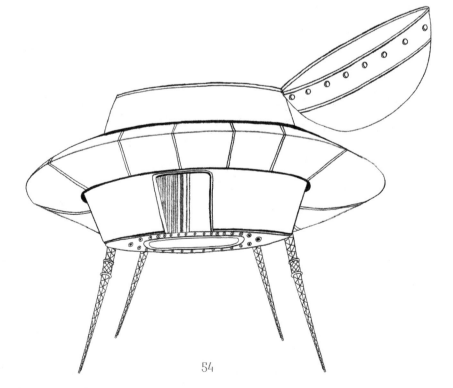

Dynamic Duos

TWO ISN'T NECESSARILY BETTER THAN ONE,
ESPECIALLY WHEN YOU FACTOR IN THE MASSIVE EGO
AND INSECURITIES OF A TYPICAL WRITER.

Connect the writers below to identify some of the most creative—
often combustible, and some short-lived—couples in literary history.

Simone de Beauvoir	Henry Miller
Mary Wollstonecraft	Ernest Hemingway
Zelda Sayre	Dashiell Hammett
Anaïs Nin	Jean-Paul Sartre
Sylvia Plath	Percy Bysshe Shelley
Martha Gellhorn	F. Scott Fitzgerald
Lillian Hellman	Ted Hughes

SOLUTION ON PAGE 106.

Le Rébellion

Connect the dots to reveal the setting
of the most heart-pumping (and flag-waving) scenes in
Victor Hugo's epic *Les Misérables*.

SOLUTION ON PAGE 96.

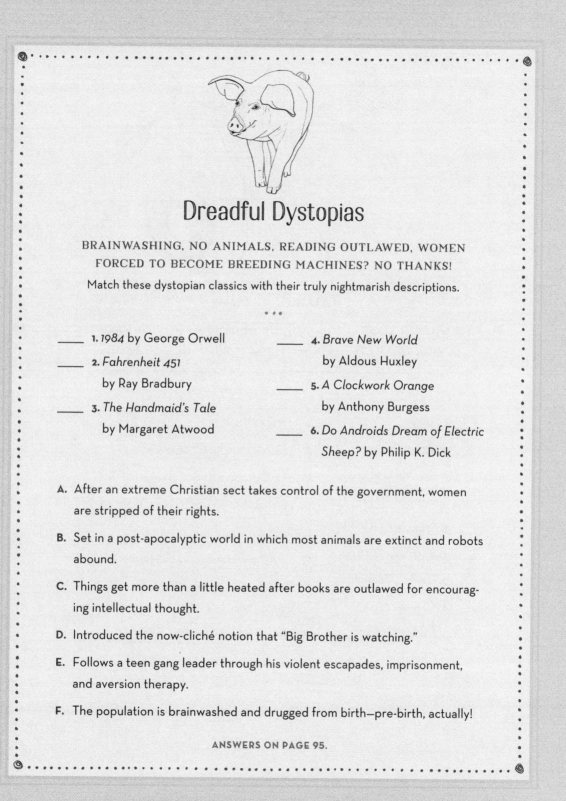

Dreadful Dystopias

BRAINWASHING, NO ANIMALS, READING OUTLAWED, WOMEN FORCED TO BECOME BREEDING MACHINES? NO THANKS!

Match these dystopian classics with their truly nightmarish descriptions.

• • •

____ **1.** *1984* by George Orwell

____ **2.** *Fahrenheit 451* by Ray Bradbury

____ **3.** *The Handmaid's Tale* by Margaret Atwood

____ **4.** *Brave New World* by Aldous Huxley

____ **5.** *A Clockwork Orange* by Anthony Burgess

____ **6.** *Do Androids Dream of Electric Sheep?* by Philip K. Dick

A. After an extreme Christian sect takes control of the government, women are stripped of their rights.

B. Set in a post-apocalyptic world in which most animals are extinct and robots abound.

C. Things get more than a little heated after books are outlawed for encouraging intellectual thought.

D. Introduced the now-cliché notion that "Big Brother is watching."

E. Follows a teen gang leader through his violent escapades, imprisonment, and aversion therapy.

F. The population is brainwashed and drugged from birth—pre-birth, actually!

ANSWERS ON PAGE 95.

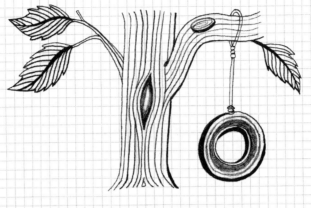

Literary Tots

IN SOME CLASSICS, KIDDOS TAKE CENTER STAGE, TUGGING AT
OUR HEARTSTRINGS WITH EACH TURN OF THE PAGE.

Match the infamous young 'uns below to the books they're featured in.

• • •

_____ **1.** Piggy

_____ **2.** Scout Finch

_____ **3.** Frankie Addams

_____ **4.** Dolores Haze

_____ **5.** Francie Nolan

_____ **6.** Ponyboy Curtis

_____ **7.** Holden Caulfield

_____ **8.** Claireece
     Precious Jones

A. *A Tree Grows in Brooklyn* by Betty Smith

B. *Lolita* by Vladimir Nabokov

C. *The Outsiders* by S. E. Hinton

D. *Lord of the Flies* by William Golding

E. *Push* by Sapphire

F. *To Kill a Mockingbird* by Harper Lee

G. *The Member of the Wedding* by
    Carson McCullers

H. *The Catcher in the Rye* by J. D. Salinger

ANSWERS ON PAGE 94.

This is the saddest story I have ever heard.

Continue the story from this intriguing first line from
Ford Madox Ford's *The Good Soldier*. Who is speaking and
why is the story sad? The possibilities are infinite.

If you run out of room, get thee to a computer
or notebook and keep going.

There's No Place Like Home

The Trojan War is over! Help the victorious Odysseus and his men navigate the seas on their arduous, years-long, and full-of-obstacles journey back to Ithaca.

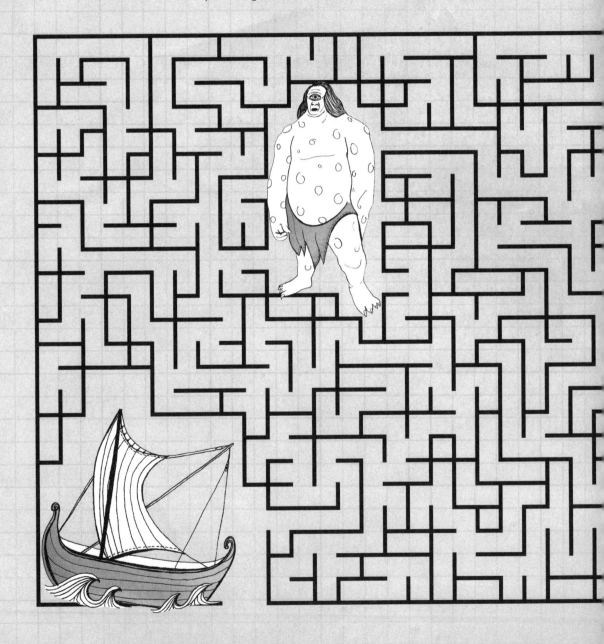

SOLUTION ON PAGE 104.

Isms

CALL YOURSELF A TRUE LIT LOVER?

Prove that you're a connoisseur of the highest caliber
by matching each ism with its definition. Writers representing
each movement should help educate any guesses.

• • •

_____ **1.** Romanticism

_____ **2.** Transcendentalism

_____ **3.** Existentialism

_____ **4.** Realism

_____ **5.** Naturalism

_____ **6.** Modernism

A. In which characters have little free will and must deal with environmental forces that are out of their control. *Writers: Theodore Dreiser, George Eliot, Thomas Hardy*

B. Meaning is derived from how characters interact with their surroundings, with an emphasis on the notion of free will. *Writers: Albert Camus, Simone de Beauvoir, Jean-Paul Sartre*

C. A focus on the individual, particularly as related to letting go of rules and restrictions and indulging the imagination. *Writers: Lord Byron, William Wordsworth, Mary and Percy Bysshe Shelley*

D. A preoccupation with the inner self and a sense of alienation, along with experimentation in style and form. *Writers: James Joyce, Virginia Woolf, T. S. Eliot*

E. Features a faithful and detailed representation of actuality, with a focus on learning through experience. *Writers: Richard Wright, Edith Wharton, Henry James*

F. Emphasis on knowledge gained through (or, ahem, *across*) contemplation and intuition. *Writers: Ralph Waldo Emerson, Henry David Thoreau, Margaret Fuller*

ANSWERS ON PAGE 95.

M Is for Macabre

ZOMBIES AND VAMPIRES AND CLOWNS, OH MY!

Test your knowledge of sleep-with-the-lights-on-after-reading tales
by completing this crossword filled with clues and answers
relating to some of literature's most horrifying works.

ACROSS

3. *The Turn of the _____*

4. Stephen King clown

6. Lovecraft's scaly, winged creature

7. "The _____ Cat" by
Edgar Allan Poe

9. *The _____ Wives*

11. "The Lottery" prize

13. *Interview with the _____*

14. Dr. Jekyll's alter ego

DOWN

1. *The Shining* hotel

2. *The Stand* villain

3. Frankenstein's occupation

5. *Rosemary's _____*

8. The Headless _____

9. *Dracula* scribe

10. "The Fall of the House
of _____"

12. *Jaws* town

SOLUTION ON PAGE 101.

Far from Home

WRITERS SURE CAN BE A RESTLESS BUNCH, MANY DECIDING
TO VENTURE BEYOND BORDERS AND TOWARD THE HORIZON.

Match the expats to the countries they settled in,
whether briefly or permanently.

Henry James	Kenya
Richard Wright	Cuba
Vladimir Nabokov	Mexico
Isak Dinesen	Morocco
Paul Bowles	England
Ernest Hemingway	United States
Elizabeth Barrett Browning	France
William S. Burroughs	Italy

SOLUTION ON PAGE 107.

Beat It

IN THE 1950s, THE BEATS STORMED ONTO THE LITERARY SCENE,
SHUNNING CONVENTION AND SOCIETAL NORMS, AND PRODUCING
SOME OF THE TWENTIETH CENTURY'S MOST ICONIC WORKS.

Track down these words—people, places, and things—associated
with the groundbreaking movement.

```
R  Z  E  M  S  N  C  M  I  H  M  F  V  T  S
H  E  K  V  B  T  J  A  C  M  E  F  I  Q  M
L  C  B  L  S  D  H  N  U  R  M  N  Z  O  U
L  K  C  E  Z  A  U  G  L  O  E  U  E  R  B
Q  R  K  Z  L  L  N  I  I  W  R  T  L  T  A
C  F  A  O  D  L  N  W  Y  L  V  E  C  L  M
Z  J  Z  E  V  G  I  O  Z  H  Y  F  K  W  R
L  Z  K  U  H  S  R  O  V  Q  Y  T  G  O  A
W  A  J  E  Y  K  F  U  N  D  Z  E  I  H  H
N  C  T  O  N  T  H  E  R  O  A  D  N  C  D
L  T  I  A  M  I  R  P  I  D  N  Y  S  M  K
I  B  H  X  Y  G  S  N  O  I  W  W  B  Y  L
O  C  S  I  C  N  A  R  F  N  A  S  E  I  B
H  D  C  V  W  R  P  G  R  F  P  E  R  C  N
M  J  E  R  I  U  R  A  I  D  P  K  G  O  G
```

Ginsberg	*Howl*	di Prima	Kerouac
On the Road	Ferlinghetti	San Francisco	jazz
New York	City Lights	LSD	
rebellion	*Dharma Bums*	*Naked Lunch*	

SOLUTION ON PAGE 110.

Book 'Em

VAGRANCY, RADICALISM, AND "INDECENCY."

Take this quiz to see if you know which offenses landed some of
literature's most revered icons in the clink.

———◆———

1. This Irish scribe served two years for "gross indecency." After his release, he
moved to France, where he died penniless at the age of forty-six.

    A. James Joyce

    B. W. B. Yates

    C. George Bernard Shaw

    D. Oscar Wilde

2. Arrested for his involvement in a progressive literary movement—perceived
to be anti-government—this Russian was sentenced to execution by a firing
squad before his sentence was reduced to four years of hard labor.

    A. Leo Tolstoy

    B. Fyodor Dostoyevsky

    C. Alexander Pushkin

    D. Anton Chekhov

3. This American referred to his thirty days spent in Buffalo's Erie County Penitentiary—for vagrancy—as "unprintable," "unthinkable," and "undescribable."

      A. Stephen Crane

      B. Herman Melville

      C. Jack London

      D. Edgar Allan Poe

4. This crime novelist—and social activist—was caught up in the Red Scare of the 1950s. After he refused to "name names" of fellow members of the radical Civil Rights Congress, he was charged with contempt and subsequently served six months in jail.

      A. Truman Capote

      B. Dashiell Hammett

      C. Raymond Chandler

      D. James M. Cain

5. In the midst of a jealousy-fueled quarrel with his lover, this French writer shot his beau, fellow writer, Arthur Rimbaud. Rimbaud survived, but the shooter still served time for the scuffle.

      A. Paul Verlaine

      B. Victor Hugo

      C. Charles Baudelaire

      D. Gustave Flaubert

ANSWERS ON PAGE 95.

Go to Town

Even with eyes protected by the green spectacles, Dorothy and her friends were at first dazzled by the brilliancy of the wonderful City. The streets were lined with beautiful houses all built of green marble and studded everywhere with sparkling emeralds. They walked over a pavement of the same green marble, and where the blocks were joined together were rows of emeralds, set closely, and glittering in the brightness of the sun. The window panes were of green glass; even the sky above the City had a green tint, and the rays of the sun were green.

• • •

Be sure to sharpen your green pencil—and have a couple of shades on hand—before coloring this vivid description of the Emerald City from L. Frank Baum's *The Wonderful Wizard of Oz*.

Marry, Kill, Do

WHILE THERE'S NO DENYING THE MAGNETISM OF A DUDE WITH
AN EXTENSIVE VOCABULARY AND A WAY WITH VERSE,
CREATIVE FIRE CAN ALSO BE, WELL, COMBUSTIBLE.

Decide which of these poets you'd like to marry,
which you'd like to kill, and which you'd like to do.

POETS	M	K	D
ROMANTICS			
Percy Bysshe Shelley			
Lord Byron			
William Wordsworth			
BEATS			
Allen Ginsberg			
Lawrence Ferlinghetti			
Jack Kerouac			
ECCENTRICS			
e e cummings			
Dylan Thomas			
James Joyce			
EARLY AMERICANS			
Edgar Allan Poe			
Walt Whitman			
Herman Melville			
MODERNISTS			
T. S. Eliot			
Wallace Stevens			
Ezra Pound			

Live or Die?

'TIS THE QUESTION THAT ALL WRITERS MUST FACE
WHEN WRAPPING UP A NARRATIVE.

Test your knowledge of lead characters' fates by identifying who survives
and who takes their last breath on the page.

CHARACTERS	LIVE	DIE
1. Isabel Archer from *The Portrait of a Lady* by Henry James		
2. Jude Fawley from *Jude the Obscure* by Thomas Hardy		
3. The narrator from *Invisible Man* by Ralph Ellison		
4. Josef K. from *The Trial* by Franz Kafka		
5. John Singer from *The Heart Is a Lonely Hunter* by Carson McCullers		
6. Humbert Humbert from *Lolita* by Vladimir Nabokov		
7. Lily Bart from *The House of Mirth* by Edith Wharton		
8. Ishmael from *Moby-Dick* by Herman Melville		

ANSWERS ON PAGE 95.

A Very Bad Omen

ON THE STORMY NIGHT BEFORE HER WEDDING
TO MR. ROCHESTER, JANE EYRE GOES FOR A WALK AND
ENCOUNTERS THE CHARRED REMNANTS OF A CHESTNUT TREE
THAT HAS BEEN STRUCK BY LIGHTNING—THE VERY TREE
WHERE THEY HAD EXPRESSED THEIR LOVE FOR ONE ANOTHER.

Sharpen your pencil and draw the bad arboreal omen
from Charlotte Brontë's *Jane Eyre*.

Noms de Plume

WHETHER TO COMBAT SEXISM, DITCH THEIR
UNMEMORABLE BIRTH NAMES, OR JUST BECAUSE, MANY
WRITERS THROUGH THE AGES HAVE ELECTED TO PUBLISH
THEIR WORKS UNDER A PEN NAME.

Match the renowned writers below to their pseudonyms.

Ricardo Neftalí Reyes Basoalto	Currer Bell
Ramona Lofton	Pablo Neruda
Charles Lutwidge Dodgson	O. Henry
Mary Anne Evans	Mark Twain
Eric Arthur Blair	George Eliot
Samuel Langhorne Clemens	George Orwell
Charlotte Brontë	Lewis Carroll
William Sydney Porter	Sapphire

SOLUTION ON PAGE 107.

Timeless Truths

CLICHÉ OR UNIVERSAL WISDOM?
TOMAYTO, TOMAHTO.

Match these literary mic-drop lines with their insightful scribes, whose words still resonate today (and will, no doubt, well into the future).

❖

1. "At a time like this, scorching irony, not convincing argument, is needed. O! had I the ability, and could reach the nation's ear, I would, to-day, pour out a fiery stream of biting ridicule, blasting reproach, withering sarcasm, and stern rebuke. For it is not light that is needed, but fire; it is not the gentle shower, but thunder. We need the storm, the whirlwind, and the earthquake."

    A. Walt Whitman

    B. Frederick Douglass

    C. Dorothy Parker

    D. W. E. B. Du Bois

2. "Reader, suppose you were an idiot. And suppose you were a member of Congress. But I repeat myself."

    A. Louisa May Alcott

    B. Edgar Allan Poe

    C. Ralph Waldo Emerson

    D. Mark Twain

3. "Not until we are lost do we begin to understand ourselves."

    A. Gertrude Stein

    B. Herman Melville

    C. Henry David Thoreau

    D. Joseph Conrad

4. "Nobody minds having what is too good for them."

    A. Virginia Woolf

    B. Oscar Wilde

    C. Edith Wharton

    D. Jane Austen

5. "That which does not kill us makes us stronger."

    A. Friedrich Nietzsche

    B. Emily Dickinson

    C. Flannery O'Connor

    D. Franz Kafka

ANSWERS ON PAGE 95.

An Unexpected Surprise

WHEN MATTHEW CUTHBERT ARRIVES AT THE BRIGHT RIVER
TRAIN STATION AT THE BEGINNING OF L. M. MONTGOMERY'S
ANNE OF GREEN GABLES, HE IS CONFUSED.

Connect the dots to reveal what awaits him.

SOLUTION ON PAGE 96.

Literary BFFs

YOU MAY HAVE ACED THE LITERARY DISSES QUIZ (PAGE 34),
BUT HOW WELL DO YOU KNOW THE WRITERLY
FRIENDSHIPS OF YESTERYEAR?

Match the pairs who had each other's backs and shared sincere
camaraderie and admiration beyond the page.

James Boswell	Edith Wharton
Truman Capote	Ernest Hemingway
Charlotte Brontë	Toni Morrison
Gertrude Stein	Harper Lee
James Baldwin	Elizabeth Gaskell
Ralph Waldo Emerson	Samuel Johnson
Henry James	Louisa May Alcott
Sylvia Plath	Anne Sexton

SOLUTION ON PAGE 108.

Banned Books Brigade

SEX, VIOLENCE, AGE INAPPROPRIATENESS—THESE ARE JUST A FEW OF THE COUNTLESS REASONS FOLKS HAVE SOUGHT TO SUPPRESS CERTAIN CLASSICS.

Test your knowledge of literature's most challenged books by completing this crossword filled with clues and answers related to banned books.

ACROSS

2. Alice Walker's titular color
5. Rowling wizard
7. *Lolita* narrator
8. *One Flew Over the Cuckoo's Nest* nurse
10. Holden Caulfield's sister
11. *Lady Chatterley's* _____
12. *Sophie's Choice* narrator
13. *Native* _____
14. *Their* _____ *Were Watching God*

DOWN

1. _____ *Place*
3. Harry Angstrom's nickname
4. *1984* foe: Big _____
6. Atticus Finch's occupation
7. *Catch-22* author
9. *Ulysses* city
12. *I Know Why the Caged Bird* _____

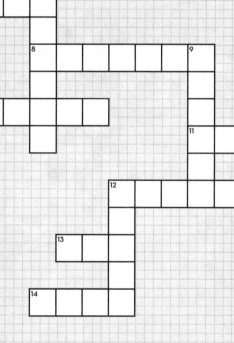

SOLUTION ON PAGE 102.

Bottom's Up

TITANIA:

I pray thee, gentle mortal, sing again:
Mine ear is much enamour'd of thy note;
So is mine eye enthralled to thy shape;
And thy fair virtue's force perforce doth move me
On the first view to say, to swear, I love thee.

Just try not to chuckle as you color in this lush, moon-lit scene
from Shakespeare's *A Midsummer Night's Dream*, in which
Titania, under a spell, becomes instantly enamored
of the recently transformed Bottom.

Write On!

One dollar and eighty-seven cents.
That was all.

So opens O. Henry's classic short story "The Gift of the Magi," a timeless tale about love, thoughtfulness . . . and d'oh moments. Continue the tale below. Who is the person who has—or needs—this particular amount of money? Why? What is the setting?

If you run out of room, get thee to a computer
or notebook and keep going.

Never the Twain Shall Meet

IT WAS MARK TWAIN WHO SAID, "NEVER PUT OFF TILL
TOMORROW WHAT YOU CAN DO THE DAY AFTER TOMORROW."

True Twain fans, however, won't likely be able to put off searching
for these words related to his life and works.

```
M D Y W C Y H U C K D N T A W
J N K O I J R I Z Q C S I H I
I V C G C T F A W F I Q I S Z
W L E K D F S L N L K T U T T
I H B L J F T L A Z E R F E L
J E I U E T U N Q W T E O A Y
I P H T C V R G A T C T N M U
M O K Z E U A S P O R I E B A
L P R N O S H R B T O R T O M
P V Q J A H U A T K E W U A L
C O L L O Q U I A L P E K T A
T Y P Q O N H G T U D P K N U
I P P I S S I S S I M Y P D V
I R U O S S I M Y M F T F K P
F M X M O T Y G Z H I C Y M D
```

white suit	Jim	travel	journalist
Tom	Mississippi	whitewash	colloquial
Huck	steamboat	Missouri	
wit	typewriter	Becky	

SOLUTION ON PAGE 111.

Southern Gothic

Accompany the Bundren family—Anse, his four sons, and one daughter,
from William Faulkner's *As I Lay Dying*—as they transport their

recently deceased matriarch, Addie, from their rural Mississippi home
to her final resting place in Jefferson.

SOLUTION ON PAGE 105.

What's Your Pen Name?

HAVING TROUBLE COMING UP WITH A WRITERLY
ALTER EGO—OR WANT TO JUST FOR FUN? THIS HIGHLY
SCIENTIFIC (NOT REALLY) PEN-NAME GENERATOR—
FEATURING SOME FAMILIAR LITERARY NAMES—WILL
HELP YOU MAKE UP YOUR MIND.

Match the initials of your first and last names to the names below.
Both female and male first names are offered and then also a last name
for both. You can also go the Robert Louis Stevenson route and
include a middle name in the mix.

———◆———

A: Agatha / Aldous / Alcott

B: Beatrix / Bram / Butler

C: Charlotte / Cormac / Conrad

D: Dorothy / Dashiell / Dickey

E: Edith / Edgar / Ellison

F: Flannery / Franz / Fitzgerald

G: Gertrude / George / Golding

H: Harper / Henry / Hawthorne

I: Iris / Ian / Irving

J: Jane / James / Jackson

K: Katherine / Kurt / Keats

L: Louisa / Langston / Longfellow

M: Maya / Mark / Maugham

N: Neale / Neil / Norman

O: Octavia / Oscar / Orwell

P: Patricia / Philip / Pynchon

Q: Quindlen / Quinn / Quick

R: Rachel / Raymond / Roth

S: Shirley / Sinclair / Steinbeck

T: Toni / Truman / Thoreau

U: Ursula / Upton / Updike

V: Virginia / Vladimir / Vonnegut

W: Willa / Walker / Whitman

X: Name of the street you grew up on

Y: Yoon / Yann / Yates

Z: Zadie / Zachary / Zola

-------------------------- -------------------------- --------------------------

First name   Middle name   Last name

What's Re(a)d All Over?

Channel any still-lingering inner teenage angst while you connect the dots to reveal one of the iconic symbols from J. D. Salinger's *The Catcher in the Rye*.

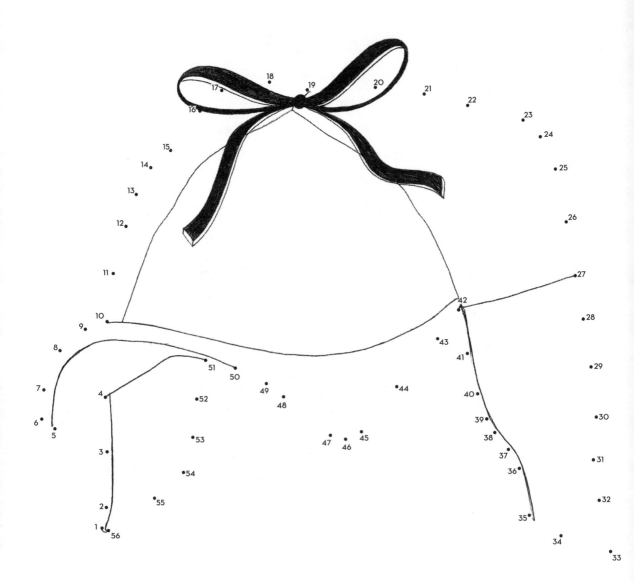

SOLUTION ON PAGE 97.

Gather 'Round

ONE OF THE MOST RENOWNED GROUPS OF LITERATI
(AND OTHER CREATIVE INTELLECTUALS), THE
ALGONQUIN ROUND TABLE BOASTED DOROTHY PARKER,
ROBERT BENCHLEY, AND ROBERT SHERWOOD AS MEMBERS.

Create your own Round Table below by drawing in six writers
you'd enjoy bantering with over a couple of cocktails.

The End

SURE, YOU MAY HAVE ACED THE FIRST-LINES QUIZ
AT THE BEGINNING OF THIS BOOK, BUT HOW WELL DO YOU
KNOW LITERATURE'S MOST ICONIC CLOSING LINES?

This is your last lit-lover's activity—relish it!

• • •

_____ **1.** *Adventures of Huckleberry Finn* by Mark Twain

_____ **2.** *Heart of Darkness* by Joseph Conrad

_____ **3.** *A Tale of Two Cities* by Charles Dickens

_____ **4.** *The Awakening* by Kate Chopin

_____ **5.** *Wuthering Heights* by Emily Brontë

_____ **6.** *Emma* by Jane Austen

_____ **7.** *My Ántonia* by Willa Cather

_____ **8.** *Frankenstein* by Mary Shelley

A. "There was the hum of bees, and the musky odor of pinks filled the air."

B. "Whatever we had missed, we possessed together the precious, the incommunicable past."

C. "He was soon borne away by the waves and lost in darkness and distance."

D. "I lingered round them, under that benign sky: watched the moths fluttering among the heath and harebells, listened to the soft wind breathing through the grass, and wondered how any one could ever imagine unquiet slumbers for the sleepers in that quiet earth."

E. "The offing was barred by a black bank of clouds, and the tranquil waterway leading to the uttermost ends of the earth flowed somber under an overcast sky—seemed to lead into the heart of an immense darkness."

F. "But I reckon I got to light out for the Territory ahead of the rest, because Aunt Sally she's going to adopt me and sivilize me and I can't stand it. I been there before."

G. "But, in spite of these deficiencies, the wishes, the hopes, the confidence, the predictions of the small band of true friends who witnessed the ceremony, were fully answered in the perfect happiness of the union."

H. "It is a far, far better thing that I do, than I have ever done; it is a far, far better rest that I go to than I have ever known."

ANSWERS ON PAGE 95.

Solutions

In the Beginning
1. C; 2. E; 3. G; 4. F; 5. H; 6. B; 7. D; 8. A

Vile Villains
1. C; 2. E; 3. B; 4. D; 5. A; 6. F

Spinster: Yea or Nay?
1. spinster; 2. spinster; 3. married; 4. spinster*; 5. spinster; 6. married;
7. married; 8. spinster; 9. married; 10. spinster; 11. spinster; 12. married

Who Played Whom?
1. D (in *Bright Star* and *In the Heart of the Sea*); 2. B (in *Sylvia*);
3. E (in *Tom & Viv*); 4. M (in *The End of the Tour*); 5. C (in *Dorothy Parker and the Vicious Circle*); 6. G (in *Becoming Jane*); 7. L (in *Shadowlands*);
8. N (in *Shakespeare in Love*); 9. I (in *Wilde*); 10. K (in *The Hours* and *Hemingway & Gellhorn*); 11. F (in *Finding Neverland*); 12. J (in *Capote*);
13. H (in *Miss Potter*); 14. A (in *Howl* and *The Broken Tower*)

Title Trivia
1. C; 2. H; 3. J; 4. D; 5. G; 6. I; 7. F; 8. B; 9. E; 10. A

Love Match
1. B; 2. A; 3. F; 4. D; 5. E; 6. C

Odd Jobs
1. F; 2. B; 3. E; 4. C; 5. D; 6. I; 7. A; 8. G; 9. H

Parting Is Such Sweet Sorrow
1. H; 2. C; 3. J; 4. F; 5. A; 6. I; 7. E; 8. G; 9. B; 10. D

Legendary Lit Disses
1. A; 2. C; 3. D; 4. C; 5. B

Shakespeare, Dickens, or Joyce?
1. Dickens, in *Bleak House*; 2. Shakespeare, in *Love's Labour's Lost*; 3. Dickens, in *The Life and Adventures of Nicholas Nickleby*; 4. Shakespeare, in *Hamlet*;

5. Joyce, in *Ulysses*; 6. Dickens, in *Great Expectations*; 7. Joyce, in *Finnegans Wake*; 8. Shakespeare, in *The Taming of the Shrew*; 9. Dickens, in *The Pickwick Papers*; 10. Joyce, in *Ulysses*

Let's Get Visual
1. *Catch-22*; 2. *The Grapes of Wrath*; 3. *The Sun Also Rises*;
4. *Heart of Darkness*; 5. *The Fountainhead*; 6. *A Clockwork Orange*;
7. *A Farewell to Arms*; 8. *Watership Down*

Literary Lotharios
1. D; 2. B; 3. A; 4. C; 5. F; 6. E

Hit or Flop?
1. flop; 2. hit; 3. flop; 4. flop; 5. hit; 6. hit; 7. flop; 8. hit; 9. flop; 10. hit

Strange Habits
1. B; 2. D; 3. E; 4. A; 5. C; 6. F

Dreadful Dystopias
1. D; 2. C; 3. A; 4. F; 5. E; 6. B

Literary Tots
1. D; 2. F; 3. G; 4. B; 5. A; 6. C; 7. H; 8. E

Isms
1. C; 2. F; 3. B; 4. E; 5. A; 6. D

Book 'Em
1. D; 2. B; 3. C; 4. B; 5. A

Live or Die?
1. live; 2. die; 3. live; 4. die; 5. die; 6. live; 7. die; 8. live

Timeless Truths
1. B; 2. D; 3. C; 4. D; 5. A

The End
1. F; 2. E; 3. H; 4. A; 5. D; 6. G; 7. B; 8. C

Dot-to-Dot

Standin' on the Dock By the Bay

Into the Woods

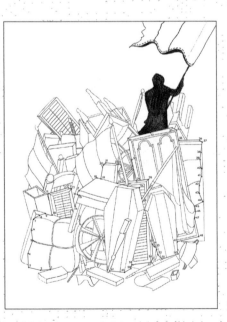

Le Rébellion

An Unexpected Surprise

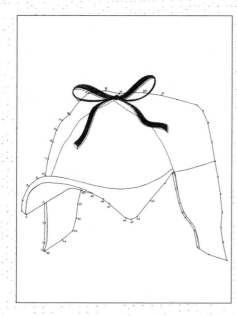

What's Re(a)d All Over?

Crosswords

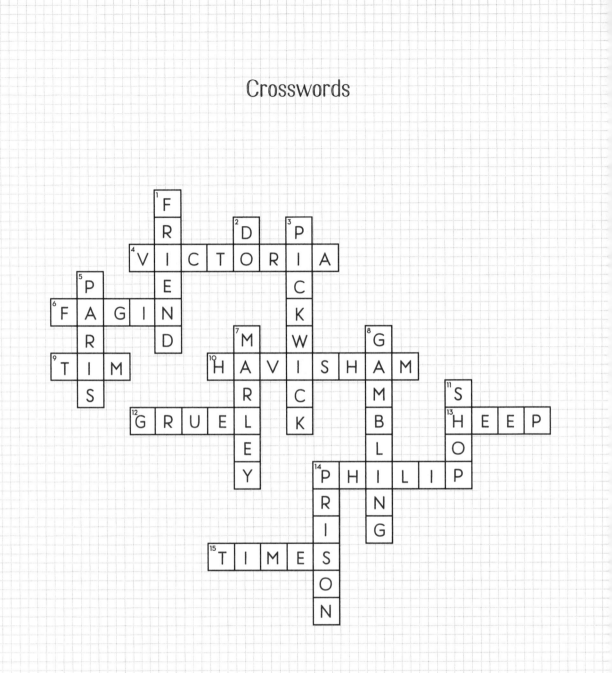

A Dickensian World

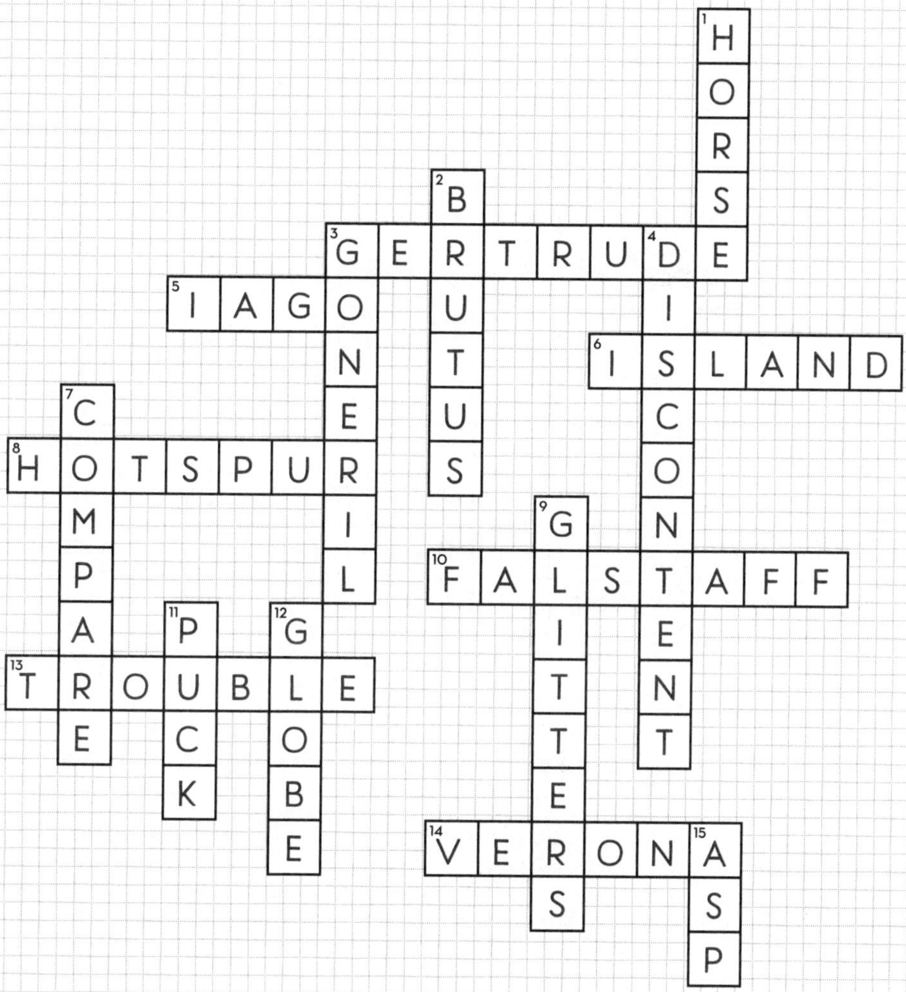
1 HORSE
2 BRUTUS
3 GERTRUDE
3 GONERIL
4 DISCONTENT
5 IAGO
6 ISLAND
7 COMPARE
8 HOTSPUR
9 GLITTERS
10 FALSTAFF
11 PUCK
12 GLOBE
13 TROUBLE
14 VERONA
15 ASP

Much Ado About Shakespeare

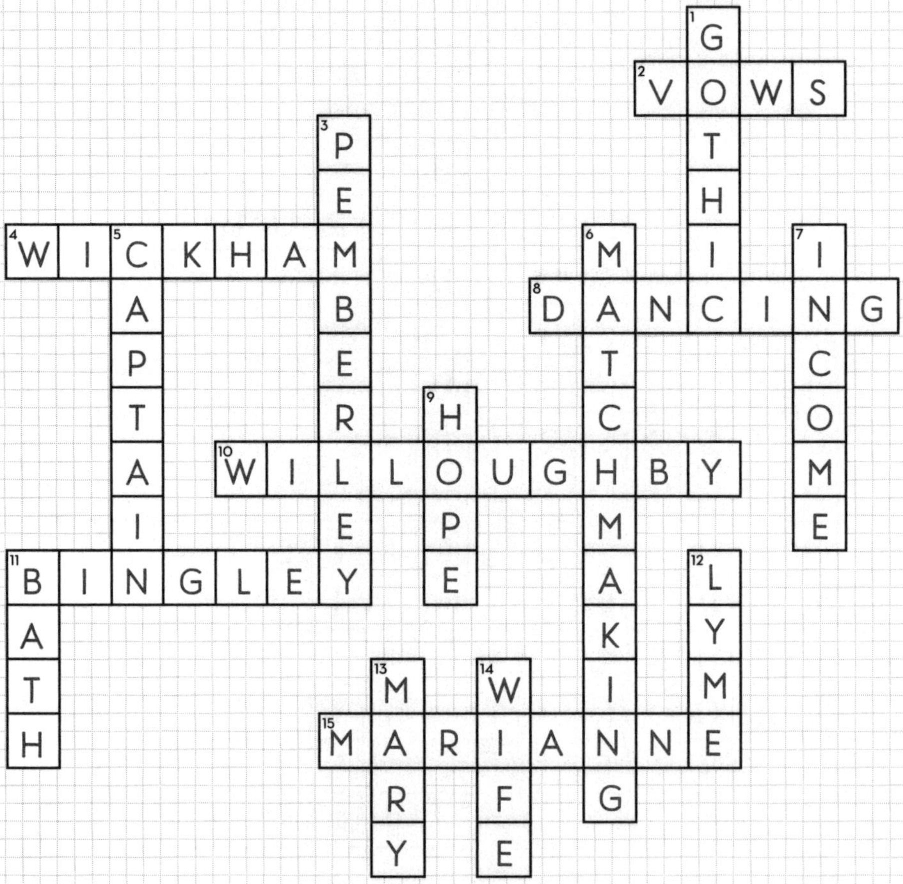
1 GOTHIC
2 VOWS
3 PEMBERLEY
4 WICKHAM
5 CAPTAIN
6 MATCHMAKING
7 INCOME
8 DANCING
9 HOPE
10 WILLOUGHBY
11 BINGLEY
11 BATH
12 LYME
13 MARY
14 WIFE
15 MARIANNE

Northanger Savvy

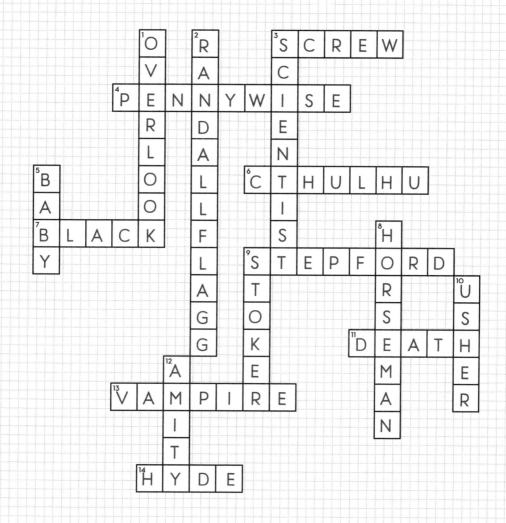

A crossword puzzle with the following answers:

Across:
3. SCREW
4. PENNYWISE
6. CTHULHU
7. BLACK
9. STEPFORD
11. DEATH
13. VAMPIRE
14. HYDE

Down:
1. OVERLOOK
2. RANDALLFLAGG
3. SCIENTIST
5. BABY
8. HORSEMAN
10. USHER
12. AMITY
Also: STOKE(R)

M Is for Macabre

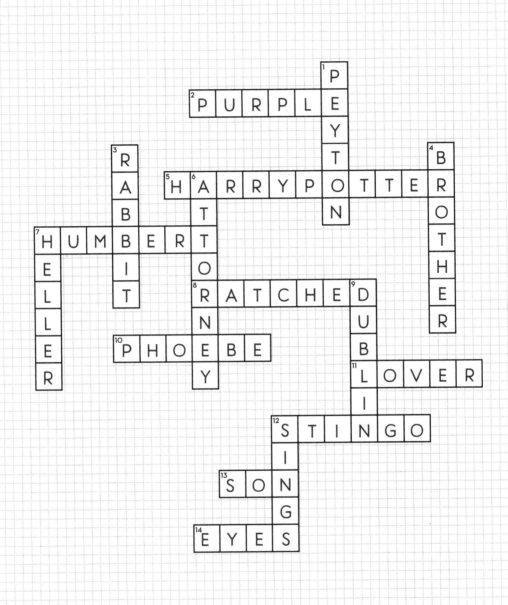

Banned Books Brigade

Mazes

There She Blows!

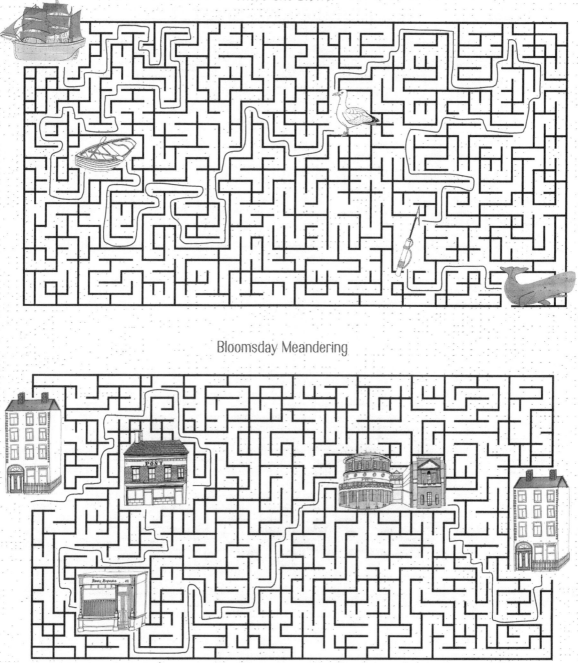

Bloomsday Meandering

On the Road

There's No Place Like Home

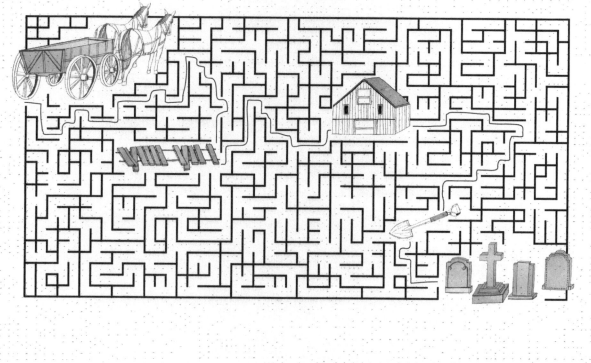

Mix and Match

War and (No) Peace

War and Peace by Leo Tolstoy	Napoleonic Wars (1803–15)
A Tale of Two Cities by Charles Dickens	French Revolution (1789–99)
All Quiet on the Western Front by Erich Maria Remarque	World War I (1914–18)
Catch-22 by Joseph Heller	World War II (1939–45)
The Last of the Mohicans by James Fenimore Cooper	French and Indian War (1754–63)
Gone with the Wind by Margaret Mitchell	American Civil War (1861–65)
For Whom the Bell Tolls by Ernest Hemingway	Spanish Civil War (1936–39)

Dynamic Duos

Simone de Beauvoir	Jean-Paul Sartre
Mary Wollstonecraft	Percy Bysshe Shelley
Zelda Sayre	F. Scott Fitzgerald
Anaïs Nin	Henry Miller
Sylvia Plath	Ted Hughes
Martha Gellhorn	Ernest Hemingway
Lillian Hellman	Dashiell Hammett

Far From Home

Henry James	◄---►	England
Richard Wright	◄---►	France
Vladimir Nabokov	◄---►	United States
Isak Dinesen	◄---►	Kenya
Paul Bowles	◄---►	Morocco
Ernest Hemingway	◄---►	Cuba
Elizabeth Barrett Browning	◄---►	Italy
William S. Burroughs	◄---►	Mexico

Noms de Plume

Ricardo Neftalí Reyes Basoalto	◄---►	Pablo Neruda
Ramona Lofton	◄---►	Sapphire
Charles Lutwidge Dodgson	◄---►	Lewis Carroll
Mary Anne Evans	◄---►	George Eliot
Eric Arthur Blair	◄---►	George Orwell
Samuel Langhorne Clemens	◄---►	Mark Twain
Charlotte Brontë	◄---►	Currer Bell
William Sydney Porter	◄---►	O. Henry

Literary BFFs

James Boswell ←---→ Samuel Johnson

Truman Capote ←---→ Harper Lee

Charlotte Brontë ←---→ Elizabeth Gaskell

Gertrude Stein ←---→ Ernest Hemingway

James Baldwin ←---→ Toni Morrison

Ralph Waldo Emerson ←---→ Louisa May Alcott

Henry James ←---→ Edith Wharton

Sylvia Plath ←---→ Anne Sexton

Word Search

Hemingway Hunt

```
K O Q W G W T A P S X P A K W
V W R B S S L A A W Z Y I O D
X F U L E E P W R A H L M X S
I M J W L A N E I K I E N H L
F P Y W P W Q R S M N L N Q H
S E Z Y E L H S A T T E R B T
K O B V M Q U N U B Z L T Y H
U Y G O A N J X H V E J V A G
N S P L X A I N M F U K P K I
I G G H R I N A Q P B D A A F
X Z R O G F N H P M Y R A J L
C A T S H O W G S S J A V N L
M A R L I N O H C A M E C G U
F J N G N X A R W H S B R T B
Z I S V S K S A Z Y N M D R H
```

A Good Word Is Hard to Find

```
C V R Q Q T D S I L Z P R T E
X A R N W S N O M O N Z N N G
Z G Q D T O S V O E W D G E R
C A T H O L I C H L C A L L E
N O I T A L E V E R B P A O V
P S R N B S Y F D N E E S I N
E A O O A C H U S A G Q S V O
C V R S I M M S C A M I E I C
X H V H O Y D O X I E L S S W
F Y T T D U C O Y A D D O B L
W O O R P K T I O R H A W H N
G N A C M P Z H P G T T Y V U
R Y J A I G R O E G L D I O J
Q F T R H T F A F R S M F M C
B A R W S L C Y X G N N K O I
```

109

Renaissance Fare

```
N R C X P R F H Z S V M V T A
C O W U E K U Y L I Y P L R Z
F K I M L G G M N S H R Q I F
L G O T H T O Z A I U I L F Q
M O W E A K U E K R R D N Y O
T O S J X R K R X C S E M I Z
B Y T W I A G C E E T C F J F
J Y Z D E T W I S H O V D U I
K P R P U D Q B M T N J I X N
M B S T S B G F B T D D R U E
G A R V E Y O Q I P A Z P G L
R F Z F F O P I Z G I E U A L
K C O L X J P J S S C E R T U
I D E N T I T Y H A A T V G C
H A M E L R A H K Y R Q Z J S
```

Beat It

```
R Z E M S N C M I H M F V T S
H E K V B T J A C M E F I Q M
L C B L S D H N U R M N Z O U
L K C E Z A U G L O E U E R B
Q R K Z L L N I I W R T L T A
C F A O D L N W Y L V E C L M
Z J Z E V G I O Z H Y F K W R
L Z K U H S R O V Q Y T G O A
W A J E Y K F U N D Z E I H H
N C T O N T H E R O A D N C D
L T I A M I R P I D N Y S M K
I B H X Y G S N O I W W B Y L
O C S I C N A R F N A S E I B
H D C V W R P G R F P E R C N
M J E R I U R A I D P K G O G
```

Never the Twain Shall Meet

```
M D Y W C Y H U C K D N T A W
J N K O I J R I Z Q C S I H I
I V C G C T F A W F I Q I S Z
W L E K D F S L N L K T U T T
I H B L J F T L A Z E R F E L
J E I U E T U N Q W T E O A Y
I P H T C V R G A T C T N M U
M O K Z E U A S P O R I E B A
L P R N O S H R B T O R T O M
P V Q J A H U A T K E W U A L
C O L L O Q U I A L P E K T A
T Y P Q O N H G T U D P K N U
I P P I S S I S S I M Y P D V
I R U O S S I M Y M F T F K P
F M X M O T Y G Z H I C Y M D
```